The Wicked Exchange

Dr Daniel Olukoya

THE WICKED EXCHANGE

A publication of
MOUNTAIN OF FIRE AND MIRACLES MINISTRIES
13, Olasimbo Street, off Olumo Road, Onike,
P. O. Box 2990, Sabo, Yaba, Lagos, Nigeria.

ISBN: 978-978-920-079-5

For further information or permission contact:
Email: pasteurdanielolukoya_french@yahoo.fr
mfmhqworldwide@mountainoffire.org

Or visit our website: www.mountainoffire.org
http://mfmbiligualbooks4evangelism.blogspot.com/

Our message entitled 'The wicked exchange' is a warfare message. In it, we would be looking at one of the wicked operations of the enemy. Therefore, I would like you to read it carefully.

THINGS TO UNDERSTAND ABOUT THE WICKED

1. If God opens your eyes to see the wicked operations of the enemy and you are able to see a little bit of what they do, you will understand what Jesus meant when He says, "*Pray without ceasing.*" They work like automatic machines. They do not rest. They do not go on holiday. They work hard at what they are doing to populate hell fire.

2. A lot of wicked operations are so strange that some people think it is superstition.

WHAT DOES IT MEAN TO FERTILIZE A THING?

It means to enrich a thing. A fertilizer is something that is used to enrich something. When you supply a thing with nourishment, you are fertilizing it. When you do something that will make another thing to germinate quickly, you are fertilizing the thing. Fertilization is also real in the spiritual realm. You can fertilize for good or for evil.

SOME QUESTIONS TO CONSIDER ON WICKED FERTILIZATION

1. Can life be used for life? Yes, it is possible. Can a person's life be used for another? The Bible says it is possible. Isaiah 42:4 says, *"Since thou wast precious in my sight, thou hast been*

honourable, and I have loved thee; therefore will I give men for thee, and people for thy life." Life can be used for life. Somebody may be killed so that another person can live. Somebody can be made poor so that another person can be rich. Somebody can be rendered a vagabond so that another person can have direction. Can life be used for life? Yes it is possible and is being done day by day. Proverbs 11:8 says, *"The righteous is delivered out of trouble and the wicked cometh in his stead."*

2. Can virtue be transferred from person to person? Is it possible to steal the intelligence and wisdom of somebody and transfer them to another person? Yes, it is possible. They are tangible items that can be moved from place to place.

Genesis 48:13 says, “And Joseph took them both, Ephraim in his right hand toward Israel's left hand, and Manasseh in his left hand towards Israel's right hand, and brought him near unto him.” Normally, the firstborn should have the right hand laid on his head and the second born should have the left hand laid on his head. But in this case, there was an exchange. Verse 14 says, “And Israel stretched out his right hand, and laid it upon Ephraim's head, which was the younger, and his left hand upon Manasseh's head, guiding his hands wittingly; for Manasseh was the firstborn.” The virtue of Manasseh was transferred to his younger brother. This is the trouble of many firstborns. Their lives have been used for lives and their virtues have been transferred.

3. Can blessing be exchanged or taken away? Yes, it has happened before. Genesis 25:30-34 says,
"And Esau said to Jacob, Feed me, I pray thee with that same red pottage; for I am faint; therefore was his name called Edom. And Jacob said; Sell me this day thy birthright. And Esau said, Behold, I am at the point to die; and what profit shall this birthright do to me? And Jacob said, Swear to me this day, and he swore unto him; and he sold his birthright unto Jacob. Then Jacob gave Esau bread and pottage of lentils; and he did eat and drink and rose up, and went his way; thus Esau despised his birthright." This man exchanged his own blessing.

4. Can promotion be stolen? Yes, it is possible. It has happened before. The

story of Jacob and Esau is also a case in point.

5. Can a man become an animal and still remain a man physically? Yes, it is possible. The life of a man can be reduced to that of an animal? The Lord did it to Nebuchadnezzar. Daniel 4:16 says,

"Let his heart be changed from man's and let a beast's heart be given unto him; and let seven times pass over him."

This is the reason behind the unreasonable behaviour of some people. Their real personalities have been transferred and an animal spirit has been given to them. When the real heart of a person is taken out and a dog's spirit is projected inside the person, the person will become an established prostitute, male or female.

6. Can problems be transferred? Yes, somebody's problem can be transferred to another person. You can lay your hands on the sick and the sickness will be transferred to you. It has happened before. 2 Kings 5:27 says, "The leprosy therefore of Naaman shall cleave unto thee ..." Look at the choice of words very well; the leprosy of the person to be transferred was specified. It was once the problem of Naaman before it was pushed to Gehazi. So, problems can be transferred.

7. Can peace, joy and love be withdrawn? Yes. The Bible says it is possible. The power of darkness can turn somebody's love for a person to hatred. Luke 10:5-6 says "*And into whatsoever house ye enter, first say, Peace be to this house. And if the*

son of peace be there, your peace shall rest upon it; if not, it shall turn to you again." Peace can move up and down.

8. Can God make a promise to a person and later withdraw it? Yes, He can. The enemy can manipulate a person to a position where the earlier promise made by the Lord is withdrawn. I Samuel 13:13 says,
   "And Samuel said to Saul, Thou hast done foolishly: thou hast not kept the commandment of the Lord thy God which he commanded thee: for now would the Lord have established thy kingdom upon Israel forever."
   The family of Saul would have been reigning in Israel forever. There would have been nothing like the house of David reigning there. Verse 14 says,

"But now thy kingdom shall not continue; the Lord hath sought him a man after his own heart, and the Lord hath commanded him to be captain over his people, because thou hast not kept that which the Lord commanded thee."
God withdrew the promise; He transferred the destiny of Saul to David. It is possible too in the negative way.

9. Is it possible for somebody to work and somebody else who did not work reap the fruit? Yes, it is possible. Isaiah 65:21-22 says,
   "And they shall build houses, and inhabit them: and they shall plant vineyards, and eat the fruit of them. They shall not build, and another inhabit; they shall not plant, and another eat..." So, it is possible to work and not reap the benefits.

10. Can one's life be demoted and wasted in order to fertilize another life? The answer is yes. In Ezekiel 13, we can see how the souls of people can be hunted down and transferred. We see how the soul of a person can be made to fly out so that another person might live. Many years ago, a certain man rushed his daughter to me. The name of the girl was Uswa. She ran mad suddenly. As I wanted to start praying for her, the Lord said, "Don't pray. Ask this man to go to his father's house and tell the father to break open the centre of his sitting room. There, he will find a small coffin. Destroy that coffin and Uswa would be well." The man broke down and cried thinking I did not want to pray for his daughter. I encouraged him to believe the word of the Lord. So, he went to his father's house and told him what the Lord said. To his amazement, his father

confirmed it. The place was broken and the small coffin was brought out. Inside the coffin was a script on which the name of Uswa was written. The idea was to terminate and waste Uswa so that her grandfather would continue to live. Immediately the coffin was destroyed there, Uswa became well. By the time her father came back, she was already taking a drink and was laughing and playing with others. An evil exchange was programmed to take place. The devil has no power to create anything but he is the most successful robber in the universe. He can steal, transfer and exchange virtues. He can exchange a person's spirit with a terrible spirit. He can do body exchange and the affected person would look older than his or her age. The presence of the person will be inviting irritation also. He can do brain exchange, where he replaces the brain of a person with that of a goat. He can do child exchange in the womb. He can do wealth exchange. He can withdraw money from one place to another. He can do hair manipulation, virtue exchange, talents exchange, partner exchange, promotion exchange, etc. He uses people's lives to do terrible things.

SIGNS TO SHOW THAT A PERSON IS BEING USED AS A WICKED FERTILIZER

1. The person will experience what is called "firstborn demotion."

2. There would be constant failure at the edge of serious breakthroughs.

3. Unexplainable health failure.

4. Brain failure.

5. The person's children would become his enemies.

6. All kinds of terrible spiritual problems will come in. The person may find it very difficult to grow in the things of God because certain things have been taken out. His virtues have been removed.

7. The person may have a low self-image.

8. The person would have terrible nightmares especially nightmares in which he sees himself serving others all the time.

9. The person will experience a life of struggle and battle always.

WAY OUT

1. Surrender your life to the Lord. There is no other way.

2. Pull down the altars of the wicked fertilization.

3. Command a reverse of what the enemy has done wrong to you.

Believers should not sit down and allow the enemy to be operating what they know is not the ordinance of God.

PRAYER POINTS

1. Every satanic obituary written against my destiny, die, in the name of Jesus.

2. Every witchcraft agent in my place of work, receive the stripes of fire, in the name of Jesus.

3. I will not go to my enemies for help, in the name of Jesus.

4. Pharaoh of my life, rush and perish in the Red sea, in the name of Jesus.

5. My Father, contend with those who contend with my destiny, in the name of Jesus.

6. Every satanic surveillance over my life, I bind you, in the name of Jesus.

7. Every witchcraft prayer targeted against my destiny, die, in the name of Jesus.

8. Every evil power of my father's house, vomit my virtues, in the name of Jesus.

9. Every power nominating me for demotion, your time is up, die, in the name of Jesus.

10. My life, refuse the handwriting of the wicked fertilizer, in the name of Jesus.

11. The timetable of my favour shall not be frustrated, in the name of Jesus.

12. The sons of strangers shall build up my wall and kings shall minister unto me, in the name of Jesus.

13. My Father, I recover by fire my birthright that I have unconsciously sold out, in the name of Jesus.

14. Every power caging my greatness, die, in the name of Jesus.

15. Every power that wants to waste my life, your time is up, die, in the name of Jesus.

16. Every dry bone of my virtues, come alive, in the name of Jesus.

17. I withdraw my virtues from the waters, in the name of Jesus.

18. Every power planning to use me as a wicked fertilizer, die, in the name of Jesus.

19. Every power planning to use my life as a wicked fertilizer, die, in the name of Jesus.

20. Every wicked replacement of my destiny, scatter, in the name of Jesus.

21. Satanic exchange of my destiny, die, in the name of Jesus.

Thank you Jesus!!!

MFM praise and worship songs

Let God arise,
Let His enemies be scattered; (*let poverty, problems, sickness etc be scattered)* x3
Let God x2
Arise
Alleluia
****

Evil plantations
Come out now in
Jesus name.
Come out !!!
****

If I be a child of God, let fire fall.
****

Arise oh God Arise x2
And fight my battles!
Arise oh Lord Arise x2
****

Elohim x2
Jehovah! You are God
Elohim x2
Jehovah! You are God
****

Immortal God, Invisible God, Immortal God, how great thou art !

****

Verily x2
You are good
Jesus you are good

****

You are Alpha and Omega, We worship you our God, you are worthy to be praised!

****

Unquestionably you are the Lord! X2
Unquestionably x2
Unquestionably you are the Lord!

****

I can see everything turning around for my favour !

****

He is a miracle working God x2
He is Alpha and Omega
He is a miracle working God

ABOUT D. K. OLUKOYA

Dr. D. K. Olukoya is the General Overseer of the Mountain of Fire and Miracles Ministries and the Battle Cry Ministries. He holds a First Class Honours Degree in Microbiology from the University of Lagos, Nigeria and a Ph.D. in Molecular Genetics from the University of Reading, United Kingdom. As a researcher, he has over eighty scientific publications to his credit. Anointed by God, Dr. Olukoya is a teacher, prophet, evangelist and preacher of the word. His life and that of his wife, Shade and their son, Elijah Toluwani, are living proofs that all power belongs to God.

ABOUT MOUNTAIN OF FIRE AND MIRACLES MINISTRIES

Mountain of Fire and Miracles Ministries, is a ministry devoted to the revival of apostolic signs, Holy Ghost fireworks and the unlimited demonstration of the power of God to deliver to the uttermost. Absolute holiness within and without, as the greatest spiritual insecticide, and a condition for heaven is taught openly. MFM is a do-it-yourself Gospel Ministry, where your hands are trained to wage war and your fingers to fight.

A brief history of Mountain of Fire and Miracles Ministries Incorporated
The Mountain of Fire and Miracles was founded in 1989. The first meeting was held at the home of Dr. D. K Olukoya and had 24

persons in attendance. The Church later moved to No. 60, Old Yaba Road, Lagos, and then to the present International Headquarters, site on 24th April, 1994. The Mountain of Fire and Miracles Ministries' Headquarters is the largest single Christian congregation in Africa, with attendance of over 200,000 in single meetings. Mountain of Fire and Miracles Ministries is a full gospel ministry devoted to the revival of apostolic signs, Holy Ghost fireworks and the unlimited demonstration of the power of God to deliver to the uttermost. Absolute holiness, within and without, as the greatest spiritual insecticide and a pre-requisite for heaven is taught openly. MFM is a do-it-yourself Gospel ministry, where your hands are trained to wage war and your fingers to do battle.

22294937

Backoffice@cashplus.com

Fax authorisation release

Send you a release code.

stating

24002108R00015

Printed in Great Britain
by Amazon